# just for kids

Publications International, Ltd.

Favorite Brand Name Recipes at www.fbnr.com

**Microwave Cooking:** Microwave ovens vary in wattage. Use the cooking times as guidelines and check for doneness before adding more time.

**Preparation/Cooking Times:** Preparation times are based on the approximate amount of time required to assemble the recipe before cooking, baking, chilling or serving. These times include preparation steps such as measuring, chopping and mixing. The fact that some preparations and cooking can be done simultaneously is taken into account. Preparation of optional ingredients and serving suggestions is not included.

# table of contents

ready...set...go!      6

grumbling tummies      26

midday munchers      56

come and get it!!      82

the best for last      102

acknowledgments      122

index      123

# ready...
# set...go!

Get those little motors revved up with great-tasting fun foods. You've got to provide enough fuel for the day, so make breakfast a high-octane meal!

# whip 'em up wacky waffles

  1½ cups biscuit baking mix
  1 cup buttermilk
  1 large egg
  1 tablespoon vegetable oil
  ½ cup "M&M's"® Semi-Sweet Chocolate Mini Baking Bits
     Powdered sugar and maple syrup

Preheat Belgian waffle iron. In large bowl combine baking mix, buttermilk, egg and oil until well mixed. Spoon about ½ cup batter into hot waffle iron. Sprinkle with about 2 tablespoons "M&M's"® Semi-Sweet Chocolate Mini Baking Bits; top with about ½ cup batter. Close lid and bake until steaming stops, 1 to 2 minutes.* Sprinkle with powdered sugar and serve immediately with maple syrup and additional "M&M's"® Semi-Sweet Chocolate Mini Baking Bits.

*Makes 4 Belgian waffles*

*Check the manufacturer's directions for recommended amount of batter and baking time.*

**Chocolate Waffles:** Use 1¼ cups biscuit baking mix, ¼ cup unsweetened cocoa powder and ½ cup sugar for biscuit baking mix. Prepare and cook as directed above.

**Tip:** These waffles make a great dessert too! Serve them with a scoop of ice cream, chocolate sauce and a sprinkle of "M&M's"® Chocolate Mini Baking Bits.

## pizza for breakfast

....................................................................................................

    1 (6½-ounce) package pizza crust mix
    1 pound BOB EVANS® Original Recipe Roll Sausage
    1 cup diced fresh or drained canned tomatoes
    8 ounces fresh mushrooms, sliced
  1½ cups (6 ounces) shredded mozzarella cheese, divided
  1½ cups (6 ounces) shredded sharp Cheddar cheese,
        divided
    4 eggs
      Salt and pepper to taste
      Salsa (optional)

Preheat oven to 350°F. Prepare crust mix according to package directions. Spread pizza dough into greased 13×9-inch baking dish, making sure dough evenly covers bottom and 2 inches up sides of dish. Crumble and cook sausage in medium skillet until browned; drain well on paper towels. Top crust with sausage, tomatoes, mushrooms, 1 cup mozzarella cheese and 1 cup Cheddar cheese. Bake 8 to 10 minutes or until crust is golden brown at edges. Remove from oven. Whisk eggs, salt and pepper in small bowl; pour over pizza. Return to oven; bake 7 to 9 minutes more or until eggs are set. Immediately sprinkle with remaining cheeses. Serve hot with salsa, if desired. Refrigerate leftovers.

*Makes 8 to 10 servings*

**Note:** Refrigerated crescent roll dough may be used instead of pizza crust mix. Seal edges together; stretch to fit baking dish.

pizza for breakfast

# sunday morning upside-down rolls

¼ cup warm water (105°F to 115°F)
1 envelope quick-rising yeast
¼ teaspoon sugar
1 cup scalded milk, slightly cooled
½ cup WESSON® Canola Oil
½ cup sugar
3 eggs, beaten
1½ teaspoons salt
4½ cups all-purpose flour
¾ cup (1½ sticks) butter, softened
2 cups packed brown sugar
1 cup maraschino cherries, chopped
1 (16-ounce) jar KNOTT'S BERRY FARM® Light Apricot
    Pineapple Preserves

Pour water into a large bowl. Sprinkle yeast, then ¼ teaspoon sugar into water; stir well. Let stand 5 to 8 minutes or until mixture is slightly foamy. Meanwhile, in a small bowl, whisk milk, Wesson® Oil, ½ cup sugar, eggs and salt until well blended. Pour milk mixture into yeast mixture; blend well. Gradually add flour to mixture; mix until smooth. Knead dough in bowl (about 5 minutes) until smooth. Add more flour if dough is sticky. Cover with towel and let rise in warm place for 30 minutes or until dough nearly doubles in size. Punch down dough once; cover.

Meanwhile, in small bowl, cream together butter and brown sugar. Spoon (be careful not to pack) 2 teaspoons of creamed sugar mixture into *each* of 24 muffin cups. Sprinkle maraschino cherries over creamed sugar mixture; then add 2 teaspoons Knott's® preserves to *each* muffin cup. Tear small pillows of dough and place on preserves, filling *each* muffin cup to the rim. Cover; let rise about 15 to 20 minutes. Preheat oven to 375°F. Bake for 12 to 15 minutes or until golden brown. Immediately invert rolls onto cookie sheet. *Do not remove rolls from muffin cups.* Allow a few minutes for preserves to drip down the sides. Lift muffin pans from rolls; cool 5 minutes. Remove muffins to wire rack. Serve warm.

*Makes 2 dozen rolls*

sunday morning upside-down rolls

# toll house® mini morsel pancakes

2½ cups all-purpose flour
1 cup (6 ounces) NESTLÉ® TOLL HOUSE® Semi-Sweet
    Chocolate Mini Morsels
1 tablespoon baking powder
½ teaspoon salt
1¾ cups milk
2 large eggs
⅓ cup vegetable oil
⅓ cup packed brown sugar
    Powdered sugar
    Fresh sliced strawberries
    Maple syrup

**COMBINE** flour, morsels, baking powder and salt in large bowl. Combine milk, eggs, vegetable oil and brown sugar in medium bowl; add to flour mixture. Stir just until moistened (batter may be lumpy).

**HEAT** griddle or skillet over medium heat; brush lightly with vegetable oil. Pour *¼ cup* of batter onto hot griddle; cook until bubbles begin to burst. Turn; continue to cook for about 1 minute longer or until golden. Repeat with *remaining* batter.

**SPRINKLE** with powdered sugar; top with strawberries. Serve with maple syrup.                    *Makes about 18 pancakes*

Pancakes are also known as flapjacks,
griddlecakes or hotcakes.

toll house® mini morsel pancakes

# biscuits 'n gravy

**BISCUITS**

PAM® No-Stick Cooking Spray
2 cups self-rising flour
2 teaspoons sugar
1½ teaspoons baking powder
¾ cup buttermilk
¼ cup WESSON® Vegetable Oil

**GRAVY**

1 pound bulk pork sausage
¼ cup all-purpose flour
2 cups milk
¼ teaspoon salt
¼ teaspoon pepper

**BISCUITS**

Preheat oven to 450°F. Lightly spray a baking sheet with PAM® Cooking Spray. In a large bowl, combine flour, sugar and baking powder; blend well. In a small bowl, whisk together buttermilk and Wesson® Oil; add to dry ingredients and mix until dough is moist but not sticky. On a lightly floured surface, knead dough lightly 4 or 5 times. Roll dough to a ¾-inch thickness; cut with a 4-inch biscuit cutter. Knead any scraps together and repeat cutting method. Place biscuits on baking sheet and bake 10 to 15 minutes or until lightly browned. Keep warm.

**GRAVY**

Meanwhile, in a large skillet, cook and crumble sausage until brown. Reserve ¼ cup of drippings in skillet; drain sausage well. Set aside. Add flour to drippings in skillet; stir until smooth. Cook over medium heat for 2 to 3 minutes or until dark brown, stirring constantly. Gradually add milk, stirring constantly until smooth and thickened. (Use more milk if necessary to achieve desired consistency.) Stir in salt, pepper and sausage; heat through. Serve over hot split biscuits.

*Makes 6 servings (2 biscuits each)*

# breakfast s'mores

½ package Kavli® muesli crispbreads, cut in half
    crosswise while still wrapped
1 apple, thinly sliced
1 nectarine, thinly sliced
1 banana, thinly sliced
¼ cup natural-style peanut butter, with oil poured off
1 tablespoon honey
1 cup mini marshmallows

Arrange 9 crispbread pieces on baking sheet. (Reserve remaining 9 pieces for tops.)

Place sliced fruit on crispbreads in thin layers* (about ½ inch high).

Mix peanut butter with honey and place ¼ teaspoon on center of each fruit layer, circling it with 2 to 3 mini marshmallows.

Bake in a 350°F oven 4 to 8 minutes or until marshmallows are melted. Place Kavli® lids on top and serve.    *Makes 9 s'mores*

*Tip: Keep fruits separate for kids' s'mores; mix fruits for teens and adults.*

# green's "dare to dip 'em" donuts

¼ cup (½ stick) butter, softened
⅓ cup granulated sugar
1 large egg
½ teaspoon vanilla extract
1¾ cups all-purpose flour, divided
1 teaspoon baking powder
1 teaspoon ground cinnamon
½ teaspoon baking soda
¼ teaspoon salt
⅓ cup buttermilk
Vegetable oil for frying
2 tablespoons powdered sugar
Chocolate Glaze (recipe follows)
½ cup "M&M's"® Chocolate Mini Baking Bits

In large bowl cream butter and granulated sugar until light and fluffy; beat in egg and vanilla. In medium bowl combine flour, baking powder, cinnamon, baking soda and salt. Alternately add one-third flour mixture and half of buttermilk to creamed mixture, ending with flour mixture. Wrap and refrigerate dough 2 to 3 hours. On lightly floured surface roll dough to ½-inch thickness. Cut into rings using 2½-inch cookie cutter; reserve donut holes. Heat about 2 inches oil to 375°F in deep-fat fryer or deep saucepan. Fry donuts, 2 to 3 at a time, about 30 seconds on each side or until golden brown. Fry donut holes 10 to 15 seconds per side or until golden brown. Remove from oil; drain on paper towels. Cool completely. Place donut holes and powdered sugar in large plastic food storage bag; seal bag. Shake bag until donut holes are evenly coated. Prepare Chocolate Glaze. Dip donuts into glaze; decorate with "M&M's"® Chocolate Mini Baking Bits. Store in tightly covered container.

*Makes 12 donuts and 12 donut holes*

## chocolate glaze

　　1 cup powdered sugar
　　1 tablespoon plus 1 teaspoon unsweetened cocoa
　　　　powder
　　1 tablespoon plus 1 teaspoon water
　　¾ teaspoon vanilla extract

In medium bowl combine powdered sugar and cocoa powder. Stir in water and vanilla; mix well.

green's "dare to dip 'em" donut

# monte cristo sandwiches

  2 tablespoons honey mustard, divided

12 thin slices white or egg bread, divided

  4 ounces sliced deli turkey breast, divided

  8 thin slices (4 ounces) Swiss cheese, divided

  4 ounces smoked sliced deli ham, divided

  2 eggs, beaten

  $\frac{1}{4}$ cup milk

  $\frac{1}{16}$ teaspoon ground nutmeg

  2 to 3 tablespoons butter or margarine

     Powdered sugar

     Strawberry or raspberry preserves

1. Preheat oven to 450°F.

2. Spread ½ teaspoon mustard over 1 side of each of 3 bread slices. Place ¼ of turkey and 1 cheese slice over mustard on 1 bread slice. Top with second bread slice, mustard side up.

3. Place ¼ of ham and 1 cheese slice on top of bread. Top with remaining bread slice, mustard side down, pressing gently together. Repeat with remaining mustard, bread, turkey, cheese and ham to make 4 sandwiches.

4. Combine eggs, milk and nutmeg in shallow dish or pie plate. Melt 1 tablespoon butter in large nonstick skillet over medium heat. Dip both sides of each sandwich briefly in egg mixture, letting excess drip back into dish.

5. Fry 1 sandwich at a time in skillet 4 minutes or until browned, turning halfway through cooking. Transfer to greased or foil-lined baking sheet. Repeat with remaining sandwiches, adding butter to skillet as needed.

6. Bake sandwiches 5 to 7 minutes or until heated through and cheese is melted. Cut each sandwich in half diagonally; sprinkle lightly with powdered sugar. Serve immediately with preserves.      *Makes 4 sandwiches*

monte cristo sandwich

## sausage pinwheels

....................................................................................................

   2 cups biscuit mix
½ cup milk
¼ cup butter or margarine, melted
1 pound BOB EVANS® Original Recipe Roll Sausage

Combine biscuit mix, milk and butter in large bowl until blended. Refrigerate 30 minutes. Divide dough into two portions. Roll out one portion on floured surface to ⅛-inch-thick rectangle, about 10×7 inches. Spread with half the sausage. Roll lengthwise into long roll. Repeat with remaining dough and sausage. Place rolls in freezer until hard enough to cut easily. Preheat oven to 400°F. Cut rolls into thin slices. Place on baking sheets. Bake 15 minutes or until golden brown. Serve hot. Refrigerate leftovers.

*Makes 48 pinwheels*

**Note:** This recipe may be doubled. Refreeze after slicing. When ready to serve, thaw slices in refrigerator and bake.

## jam french toast triangles

....................................................................................................

   ¼ cup preserves, any flavor
6 slices whole wheat bread, divided
6 tablespoons EGG BEATERS®
¼ cup skim milk
2 tablespoons FLEISCHMANN'S® Original Margarine
1 tablespoon sugar
¼ teaspoon ground cinnamon

Evenly divide and spread preserves on 3 bread slices; top with remaining bread slices to make 3 sandwiches, pressing to seal. Cut each sandwich diagonally in half. In shallow bowl, combine Egg Beaters® and skim milk. Dip each sandwich in egg mixture to coat.

In skillet or on griddle, over medium-high heat, brown sandwiches in margarine until golden brown on both sides. Combine sugar and cinnamon; sprinkle over sandwiches. Garnish as desired and serve warm.          *Makes 6 pieces*

sausage pinwheels

# snacking surprise muffins

1½ cups all-purpose flour
1 cup fresh or frozen blueberries
½ cup sugar
2½ teaspoons baking powder
1 teaspoon ground cinnamon
¼ teaspoon salt
1 egg, beaten
⅔ cup buttermilk
¼ cup margarine or butter, melted
3 tablespoons peach preserves

**TOPPING**
1 tablespoon sugar
¼ teaspoon ground cinnamon

1. Preheat oven to 400°F. Line 12 medium muffin cups with paper liners; set aside.

2. Combine flour, blueberries, ½ cup sugar, baking powder, 1 teaspoon cinnamon and salt in medium bowl. Combine egg, buttermilk and margarine in small bowl. Add to flour mixture; mix just until moistened.

3. Spoon about 1 tablespoon batter into each muffin cup. Drop a scant teaspoonful of preserves into center of batter in each cup; top with remaining batter.

4. Combine 1 tablespoon sugar and ¼ teaspoon cinnamon in small bowl; sprinkle evenly over tops of batter.

5. Bake 18 to 20 minutes or until lightly browned. Remove muffins to wire rack to cool completely.      *Makes 12 muffins*

snacking surprise muffins

# tooty fruitys

**1 package (10 ounces) extra-light flaky biscuits
10 (1½-inch) fruit pieces, such as plum, apple, peach or
     pear
1 egg white
1 teaspoon water
  Powdered sugar (optional)**

1. Preheat oven to 425°F. Spray baking sheets with nonstick cooking spray; set aside.

2. Separate biscuits. Place on lightly floured surface. Roll with lightly floured rolling pin or flatten dough with fingers to form 3½-inch circles. Place 1 fruit piece in center of each circle. Bring 3 edges of dough up over fruit; pinch edges together to seal. Place on prepared baking sheet.

3. Beat egg white with water in small bowl; brush over dough.

4. Bake until golden brown, 10 to 15 minutes. Remove to wire rack to cool. Serve warm or at room temperature. Sprinkle with powdered sugar, if desired, just before serving.

*Makes 10 servings*

**Sweet Tooty Fruitys:** Prepare dough circles as directed. Gently press both sides of dough circles into granulated or cinnamon-sugar to coat completely. Top with fruit and continue as directed, except do not brush with egg white mixture or sprinkle with powdered sugar.

**Cheesy Tooty Fruitys:** Prepare dough circles as directed. Top each circle with ½ teaspoon softened reduced-fat cream cheese in addition to fruit. Continue as directed.

tooty fruitys

# grumbling tummies

When your kids' tummies start grumbling and it's not quite mealtime, try some of these snacks to bridge the gap between meals.

# rock 'n' rollers

4 (6- to 7-inch) flour tortillas
4 ounces Neufchâtel cheese, softened
⅓ cup peach preserves
1 cup (4 ounces) shredded fat-free Cheddar cheese
½ cup packed washed fresh spinach leaves
3 ounces thinly sliced regular or smoked turkey breast

1. Spread each tortilla evenly with 1 ounce Neufchâtel cheese; cover with thin layer of preserves. Sprinkle with Cheddar cheese.

2. Arrange spinach leaves and turkey over Cheddar cheese. Roll up tortillas; trim ends. Cover and refrigerate until ready to serve.

3. Cut "rollers" crosswise in half or diagonally into 1-inch pieces. *Makes 4 servings*

**Sassy Salsa Rollers:** Substitute salsa for peach preserves and shredded iceberg lettuce for spinach leaves.

**Ham 'n' Apple Rollers:** Omit peach preserves and spinach leaves. Substitute lean ham slices for turkey. Spread tortillas with Neufchâtel cheese as directed; sprinkle with Cheddar cheese. Top each tortilla with about 2 tablespoons finely chopped apple and 2 ham slices; roll up. Continue as directed.

**Wedgies:** Prepare Rock 'n' Rollers or any variation as directed, but do not roll up. Top with second tortilla; cut into wedges. Continue as directed.

# s'mores on a stick

1 (14-ounce) can EAGLE BRAND® Sweetened
    Condensed Milk (NOT evaporated milk), divided
1½ cups milk chocolate mini chips, divided
1 cup miniature marshmallows
11 whole graham crackers, halved crosswise
    Toppings: chopped peanuts, mini candy-coated
        chocolate pieces, sprinkles

1. Microwave half of Eagle Brand in microwave-safe bowl at HIGH (100% power) 1½ minutes. Stir in 1 cup chips until smooth; stir in marshmallows.

2. Spread chocolate mixture evenly by heaping tablespoonfuls onto 11 graham cracker halves. Top with remaining graham cracker halves; place on waxed paper.

3. Microwave remaining Eagle Brand at HIGH (100% power) 1½ minutes; stir in remaining ½ cup chips, stirring until smooth. Drizzle mixture over cookies and sprinkle with desired toppings.

4. Let stand for 2 hours; insert a wooden craft stick into center of each cookie.                    *Makes 11 servings*

**Prep Time:** 10 minutes
**Cook Time:** 3 minutes

s'mores on a stick

# cinnamon trail mix

        2 cups corn cereal squares
        2 cups whole wheat cereal squares or whole wheat
            cereal squares with mini graham crackers
    1½ cups fat-free oyster crackers
        ½ cup broken sesame snack sticks
        2 tablespoons margarine or butter, melted
        1 teaspoon ground cinnamon
        ¼ teaspoon ground nutmeg
        ½ cup bite-size fruit-flavored candy pieces

1. Preheat oven to 350°F. Spray 13×9-inch baking pan with nonstick cooking spray.

2. Place cereals, oyster crackers and sesame sticks in prepared pan; mix lightly.

3. Combine margarine, cinnamon and nutmeg in small bowl; mix well. Drizzle evenly over cereal mixture; toss to coat.

4. Bake 12 to 14 minutes or until golden brown, stirring gently after 6 minutes. Cool completely. Stir in candies.

*Makes 8 (¾-cup) servings*

## FOOD CLUES

Cinnamon comes from the dried bark of various laurel trees. The outer bark is peeled away, then the inner bark is rolled, pressed and dried.

cinnamon trail mix

# banana freezer pops

    2 ripe medium bananas
    1 can (6 ounces) frozen orange juice concentrate,
        thawed (¾ cup)
    ¼ cup water
    1 tablespoon honey
    1 teaspoon vanilla
    8 (3-ounce) paper or plastic cups
    8 wooden sticks

1. Peel bananas; break into chunks. Place in food processor or blender container.

2. Add orange juice concentrate, water, honey and vanilla; process until smooth.

3. Pour banana mixture evenly into cups. Cover top of each cup with small piece of aluminum foil. Insert wooden stick through center of foil into banana mixture.

4. Place cups on tray; freeze until firm, about 3 hours. To serve, remove foil; tear off paper cups (or slide out of plastic cups). *Makes 8 servings*

**Peppy Purple Pops:** Omit honey and vanilla. Substitute grape juice concentrate for orange juice concentrate.

**Frozen Banana Shakes:** Increase water to 1½ cups. Prepare fruit mixture as directed. Add 4 ice cubes; process on high speed until mixture is thick and creamy. Makes 3 servings.

banana freezer pops

## clown-around cones

4 waffle cones
½ cup "M&M's"® Chocolate Mini Baking Bits, divided
   Prepared decorator icing
½ cup hot fudge ice cream topping, divided
4 cups any flavor ice cream, softened
1 (1.5- to 2-ounce) chocolate candy bar, chopped
¼ cup caramel ice cream topping

Decorate cones as desired with "M&M's"® Chocolate Mini Baking Bits, using decorator icing to attach; let set. For each cone, place 1 tablespoon hot fudge topping in bottom of cone. Sprinkle with 1 teaspoon "M&M's"® Chocolate Mini Baking Bits. Layer with ¼ cup ice cream; sprinkle with ¼ of candy bar. Layer with ¼ cup ice cream; sprinkle with 1 teaspoon "M&M's"® Chocolate Mini Baking Bits. Top with 1 tablespoon caramel topping and remaining ½ cup ice cream. Wrap in plastic wrap and freeze until ready to serve. Just before serving, top each ice cream cone with 1 tablespoon hot fudge topping; sprinkle with remaining "M&M's"® Chocolate Mini Baking Bits. Serve immediately.

*Makes 4 servings*

Ice cream is often too hard to scoop when it's right out of the freezer. So when everybody is screaming for ice cream, here's how to serve it up fast! Place a 1-quart container of hard-packed ice cream in the microwave and heat at MEDIUM (50% power) about 20 seconds or just until softened.

clown-around cones

# double peanut clusters

1⅔ cups (10-ounce package) REESE'S® Peanut Butter
    Chips
1 tablespoon shortening (do not use butter, margarine,
    spread or oil)
2 cups salted peanuts

1. Line cookie sheet with waxed paper.

2. Place peanut butter chips and shortening in large microwave-safe bowl. Microwave at HIGH (100%) 1½ minutes; stir until chips are melted and mixture is smooth. If necessary, microwave an additional 30 seconds until chips are melted when stirred. Stir in peanuts.

3. Drop by rounded teaspoons onto prepared cookie sheet. (Mixture may also be dropped into small candy paper cups.) Cool until set. Store in a cool, dry place.

*Makes about 2½ dozen snacks*

**Butterscotch Nut Clusters:** Follow above directions, substituting 1⅔ cups (10-ounce package) HERSHEY'S Butterscotch Chips.

double peanut clusters

## quick pizza snacks

3 English muffins, split and toasted
1 can (14½ ounces) Italian-style diced tomatoes, undrained
¾ cup (3 ounces) shredded Italian cheese blend
Bell pepper strips (optional)

Preheat oven to 350°F. Place English muffin halves on ungreased baking sheet. Top each muffin with ¼ cup tomatoes; sprinkle with 2 tablespoons cheese. Bake about 5 minutes or until cheese is melted and lightly browned. Garnish with bell pepper strips, if desired.     *Makes 6 servings*

## backyard s'mores

2 milk chocolate bars (1.55 ounces each), cut in half
8 large marshmallows
4 whole graham crackers (8 squares)

Place each chocolate bar half and 2 marshmallows between 2 graham cracker squares. Wrap in lightly greased foil. Place on grill over medium-low KINGSFORD® Briquets about 3 to 5 minutes or until chocolate and marshmallows are melted. (Time will vary depending upon how hot coals are and whether grill is open or covered.)     *Makes 4 servings*

quick pizza snacks

# cheese straws

½ cup (1 stick) butter, softened
⅛ teaspoon salt
    Dash ground red pepper
1 pound sharp Cheddar cheese, shredded, at room
    temperature
2 cups self-rising flour

Heat oven to 350°F. In mixer bowl, beat butter, salt and pepper until creamy. Add cheese; mix well. Gradually add flour, mixing until dough begins to form a ball. Form dough into ball with hands. Fit cookie press with small star plate; fill with dough according to manufacturer's directions. Press dough onto cookie sheets in 3-inch-long strips (or desired shapes). Bake 12 minutes, just until lightly browned. Cool completely on wire rack. Store tightly covered.

*Makes about 10 dozen*

Favorite recipe from *Southeast United Dairy Industry Association, Inc.*

cheese straws

# hershey's easy chocolate cracker snacks

1⅔ cups (10-ounce package) HERSHEY'S Mint Chocolate Chips*

2 cups (12-ounce package) HERSHEY'S Semi-Sweet Chocolate Chips

2 tablespoons shortening (do not use butter, margarine, spread or oil)

60 to 70 round buttery crackers (about one-half 1-pound box)

*2 cups (11.5-ounce package) HERSHEY'S Milk Chocolate Chips and ¼ teaspoon pure peppermint extract can be substituted for mint chocolate chips.

1. Line several trays or cookie sheets with waxed paper.

2. Place mint chocolate chips, chocolate chips and shortening in large microwave-safe bowl. Microwave at HIGH (100%) 1 minute; stir. Continue heating 30 seconds at a time, stirring after each heating, until chips are melted and mixture is smooth when stirred.

3. Drop crackers into chocolate mixture one at a time. Using tongs, push cracker into chocolate so that it is covered completely. (If chocolate begins to thicken, reheat 10 to 20 seconds in microwave.) Remove from chocolate, tapping lightly on edge of bowl to remove excess chocolate. Place on prepared tray. Refrigerate until chocolate hardens, about 20 minutes. For best results, store tightly covered in refrigerator. *Makes about 5½ dozen cookies*

**Peanut Butter and Milk Chocolate:** Use 1⅔ cups (10-ounce package) REESE'S® Peanut Butter Chips, 2 cups (11.5-ounce package) HERSHEY'S Milk Chocolate Chips and 2 tablespoons shortening. Proceed as above.

**Chocolate Raspberry:** Use 1⅔ cups (10-ounce package) HERSHEY'S Raspberry Chips, 2 cups (11.5-ounce package) HERSHEY'S Milk Chocolate Chips and 2 tablespoons shortening. Proceed as above.

**White Chip and Toffee:** Melt 1⅔ cups (10-ounce package) HERSHEY'S Premier White Chips and 1 tablespoon shortening. Dip Crackers; before coating hardens sprinkle with SKOR® English Toffee Bits or HEATH® BITS 'O BRICKLE® Almond Toffee Bits.

hershey's easy chocolate cracker snacks

## kool-pop treat

1 (3-ounce) bag ORVILLE REDENBACHER'S® Microwave
 Popping Corn, popped according to package
 directions
2 cups brightly colored puffed oat cereal, such as fruit
 flavored loops
2 cups miniature marshmallows
1 (.35-ounce) package strawberry soft drink mix
2 tablespoons powdered sugar

1. In large bowl, combine popcorn, cereal and marshmallows.

2. Combine drink mix and powdered sugar; sift over popcorn
mixture. Toss to coat.   *Makes 12 (1-cup) servings*

## cheesy barbecued bean dip

½ cup canned vegetarian baked beans
3 tablespoons pasteurized process cheese spread
2 tablespoons regular or hickory smoke barbecue sauce
 Green onion piece and red bell pepper triangles, for
 garnish (optional)
2 large carrots, cut into diagonal slices
1 medium red or green bell pepper, cut into chunks

1. Place beans in small microwavable bowl; mash slightly with
fork. Stir in process cheese spread and barbecue sauce. Cover
with vented plastic wrap.

2. Microwave at HIGH 1 minute; stir. Microwave additional
30 seconds or until hot. Garnish with green onion piece and
bell pepper triangles, if desired. Serve with carrot slices and
bell pepper chunks.   *Makes 4 servings*

# old-fashioned caramel apples

1 package (14 ounces) caramels, unwrapped
2 tablespoons water
6 wooden craft sticks
6 medium Granny Smith apples
   Chopped toasted pecans, walnuts or roasted peanuts
   Orange and black jimmies or sprinkles

1. Place caramels and water in medium heavy saucepan. Cook over medium-low heat until melted and very hot, stirring frequently.

2. Insert stick into stem end of each apple. Place pecans in shallow bowl and jimmies in another shallow bowl. Dip apple into caramel, tilting saucepan until apple is coated; let excess caramel drip back in saucepan. Remove excess caramel by scraping bottom of apple across rim of saucepan. Immediately roll apple in pecans and/or jimmies. Place, stick side up, on baking sheet lined with waxed paper. Repeat with remaining apples. Rewarm caramel, if needed. Chill at least 10 minutes or until caramel is firm before serving.          *Makes 6 servings*

## FOOD CLUES

Granny Smith apples, originally developed in
Australia, are tart green apples with tough skins
and a firm, crunchy texture. They are a good choice
for eating raw and for making pies.

# brontosaurus bites

　　4 cups air-popped popcorn
　　2 cups mini-dinosaur grahams
　　2 cups corn cereal squares
　1½ cups dried pineapple wedges
　　1 package (6 ounces) dried fruit bits
　　　Butter-flavored nonstick cooking spray
　　1 tablespoon plus 1½ teaspoons sugar
　1½ teaspoons ground cinnamon
　　½ teaspoon ground nutmeg
　　1 cup yogurt-covered raisins

1. Preheat oven to 350°F. Combine popcorn, grahams, cereal, pineapple and fruit bits in large bowl; mix lightly. Transfer to 15×10-inch jelly-roll pan. Spray mixture generously with cooking spray.

2. Combine sugar, cinnamon and nutmeg in small bowl. Sprinkle ½ of sugar mixture over popcorn mixture; toss lightly to coat. Spray mixture again with additional cooking spray. Add remaining sugar mixture; mix lightly.

3. Bake snack mix 10 minutes, stirring after 5 minutes. Cool completely in pan on wire rack. Add raisins; mix lightly.

*Makes 12 (¾-cup) servings*

**Gorilla Grub:** Substitute plain raisins for the yogurt-covered raisins and ¼ cup grated Parmesan cheese for the sugar, cinnamon and nutmeg.

**Cook's Tip:** For individual party take-home treats, wrap snack mix in festive colored paper napkins.

brontosaurus bites

# tortellini teasers

Zesty Tomato Sauce (recipe follows)
½ (9-ounce) package refrigerated cheese tortellini
1 large red or green bell pepper, cut into 1-inch pieces
2 medium carrots, peeled and sliced ½ inch thick
1 medium zucchini, sliced ½ inch thick
12 medium fresh mushrooms
12 cherry tomatoes

1. Prepare Zesty Tomato Sauce; keep warm.

2. Cook tortellini according to package directions; drain.

3. Alternate 1 tortellini and 2 to 3 vegetable pieces on long frilled toothpicks or wooden skewers. Serve as dippers with tomato sauce. *Makes 6 servings*

## zesty tomato sauce

1 can (15 ounces) tomato purée
2 tablespoons finely chopped onion
2 tablespoons chopped fresh parsley
1 teaspoon dried oregano leaves
¼ teaspoon dried thyme leaves
¼ teaspoon salt
⅛ teaspoon black pepper

Combine tomato purée, onion, parsley, oregano and thyme in small saucepan. Heat thoroughly, stirring occasionally. Stir in salt and pepper. Garnish with carrot curl, if desired.

tortellini teasers

# granola crisp topping with fruit

⅓ cup old-fashioned rolled oats, uncooked
3 tablespoons chopped walnuts
¼ cup honey
1 egg white
¼ teaspoon vanilla
¼ teaspoon ground cinnamon
   Dash salt
2 cups nonfat plain or vanilla yogurt
2 cups mixed berries

Combine oats and walnuts in medium bowl. Mix together honey, egg white, vanilla, cinnamon and salt in small bowl until well blended. Add honey mixture to oats; stir until well blended. Line 11×17-inch baking sheet with foil; spray with nonstick cooking spray. Spread oat mixture in even layer on prepared baking sheet. Bake at 325°F 15 to 17 minutes or until golden brown, tossing mixture 3 to 4 times during baking. Remove from oven. Cool completely until crisp and crunchy. Serve over yogurt and berries.     *Makes 4 servings*

Favorite recipe from **National Honey Board**

granola crisp topping with fruit

# cherry-peach pops

⅓ cup peach or apricot nectar
1 teaspoon unflavored gelatin
1 (15-ounce) can sliced peaches in light syrup, drained
1 (6- or 8-ounce) carton fat-free, sugar-free peach or cherry yogurt
1 (6- or 8-ounce) carton fat-free, sugar-free cherry yogurt

1. Combine nectar and unflavored gelatin in small saucepan; let stand 5 minutes. Heat and stir over low heat just until gelatin dissolves.

2. Combine nectar mixture, peaches and yogurts in food processor. Cover and process until smooth.

3. Pour into 7 (3-ounce) paper cups, filling each about ⅔ full. Place in freezer; freeze 1 hour. Insert wooden stick into center of each cup. Freeze at least 3 more hours.

4. Let stand at room temperature 10 minutes before serving. Tear away paper cups to serve.          *Makes 7 servings*

## FOOD CLUES

Powdered gelatin will last indefinitely if it is
wrapped airtight and stored in a cool, dry place.

# sweet and sour hot dog bites

¼ **cup prepared mustard**
½ **cup SMUCKER'S® Grape Jelly**
 1 **tablespoon sweet pickle relish**
½ **pound frankfurters, cooked**

In a saucepan, combine mustard, SMUCKER'S® jelly, and relish.

Heat over very low heat, stirring constantly, until mixture is hot and well blended.

Slice frankfurters diagonally into bite-size pieces. Add to sauce and heat thoroughly. *Makes 20 snack servings*

sweet and sour hot dog bites

## sweet nothings trail mix

    5 cups rice and corn cereal squares
1½ cups raisins
1½ cups small thin pretzel sticks, broken into pieces
    1 cup candy-coated chocolate pieces
    1 cup peanuts

1. Have children decorate small resealable food storage bags with Valentine's Day stickers, if desired.

2. Combine cereal, raisins, pretzels, chocolate pieces and peanuts in large resealable plastic food storage bag; shake well. Distribute evenly among decorated bags or serve in large bowl.                                                    *Makes 10 cups*

**Serve It With Style!:** To use this recipe as a party favor, wrap handfuls of trail mix in pink plastic wrap and tie with red, white or pink ribbons.

**Prep and Cook Time:** 10 minutes

sweet nothings trail mix

# midday munchers

Lunchtime doesn't have to be a battle. With fun recipes like Chili Dogs, Monster Sandwiches and Chunky Joes, it's easy to make midday meals fun for everyone.

# tacos olé

   1 pound ground beef or turkey
   1 cup salsa
   ¼ cup *Frank's® RedHot®* Original Cayenne Pepper Sauce
   2 teaspoons chili powder
   8 taco shells, heated
      Garnish: chopped tomatoes, shredded lettuce, sliced
         olives, sour cream, shredded cheese

1. Cook beef in skillet over medium-high heat 5 minutes or until browned, stirring to separate meat; drain. Stir in salsa, **Frank's RedHot** Sauce and chili powder. Heat to boiling. Reduce heat to medium-low. Cook 5 minutes, stirring often.

2. To serve, spoon meat mixture into taco shells. Splash on more **Frank's RedHot** Sauce to taste. Garnish as desired.

*Makes 4 servings*

**Prep Time:** 5 minutes
**Cook Time:** 10 minutes

# bologna "happy faces"

4 slices whole wheat or rye bread
1 cup prepared oil and vinegar based coleslaw
8 ounces HEBREW NATIONAL® Sliced Lean Beef Bologna
  or Lean Beef Salami
4 large pimiento-stuffed green olives
  HEBREW NATIONAL® Deli Mustard

For each sandwich, spread 1 bread slice with 3 tablespoons coleslaw; top with 5 slices bologna. Cut olives in half crosswise; place over bologna for "eyes." Draw smiley "mouth" with mustard. Drop 1 tablespoon coleslaw at top of face for "hair."  *Makes 4 open-faced sandwiches*

# peanut butter and jelly club sandwich

3 tablespoons JIF® Creamy Peanut Butter
3 slices bread
2 tablespoons SMUCKER'S® Strawberry Jam
½ banana, sliced
2 strawberries, sliced

1. Spread JIF® peanut butter on 2 slices of bread. Spread SMUCKER'S® Strawberry Jam on the remaining slice of bread.

2. Place sliced banana on top of 1 slice of bread with JIF® peanut butter. Place sliced strawberries on top of other piece of bread with JIF® peanut butter.

3. Put piece of bread with strawberries on top of bread with bananas. Close sandwich with slice of bread with SMUCKER'S® Strawberry Jam facing down.  *Makes 1 serving*

bologna "happy faces"

# barbecue flying saucers with vegetable martians

½ teaspoon black pepper*
1 (10-ounce) pork tenderloin*
¼ cup barbecue sauce
½ teaspoon prepared mustard
1 (7½-ounce) package (10) refrigerated buttermilk
   biscuits
1 egg yolk (optional)
1 teaspoon water (optional)
3 to 4 drops food coloring (optional)
   Vegetable Martians (recipe follows)

*Substitute 10 ounces lean deli roasted pork for pork tenderloin and pepper, if desired.

1. Preheat oven to 425°F. Rub pepper on outside of pork tenderloin. Place pork in shallow roasting pan. Roast 15 to 25 minutes or until meat thermometer inserted into thickest part of meat registers 160°F. Remove from oven; let stand 5 minutes. Shred pork.

2. *Reduce oven temperature to 400°F.* Stir together barbecue sauce and mustard. Toss with shredded pork.

3. Roll each biscuit on lightly floured surface into 4-inch circle. Place one fifth of pork mixture on each of five circles. Moisten edges. Top with remaining biscuit circles. Crimp edges to seal.

4. Stir together egg yolk, water and food coloring to make egg-wash paint, if desired. Using clean paintbrush, paint desired designs on biscuit "flying saucers." Place on baking sheet. Bake 11 to 13 minutes or until golden. Serve with Vegetable Martians. *Makes 5 servings*

## vegetable martians

10 cherry tomatoes, baby pattypan squash or combination
5 to 10 thin slices cucumber or zucchini
¼ teaspoon reduced-fat soft cream cheese or mustard
5 to 8 currants, cut into halves
10 chow mein noodles

Skewer vegetables on toothpicks to form martian bodies. Use cream cheese to make eyes or to attach currants for eyes and mouths. Press 2 chow mein noodles into top of each martian for antennae. Remove toothpicks before serving.

*Makes 5 martians*

barbecue flying saucers with vegetable martian

# sloppy joes

1 pound ground beef or turkey
1 can (10¾ ounces) condensed tomato soup
2 tablespoons *French's*® Worcestershire Sauce
4 large rolls, split
   Garnish: shredded Cheddar cheese, sliced green
      onions, chopped tomatoes

1. Cook beef in large skillet until browned; drain. Add soup,
*¼ cup water* and Worcestershire. Heat to boiling. Simmer over
low heat 5 minutes, stirring often.

2. Serve in rolls. Top with cheese, onions and tomatoes.

*Makes 4 servings*

**Prep Time:** 5 minutes
**Cook Time:** 10 minutes

# hero spam™ sandwich

1 (16-ounce) loaf Italian bread
2 tablespoons Italian salad dressing
1 (12-ounce) can SPAM® Classic, thinly sliced
1 tomato, thinly sliced
6 ounces sliced provolone cheese
2-3 PELOPONNESE® Roasted Sweet Red Peppers *or* 1 red
      bell pepper, cut into thin rings
1 small red onion, thinly sliced
10 PELOPONNESE® pitted Kalamata olives, halved
   Lettuce leaves

Cut bread in half lengthwise; remove a portion of soft center. Drizzle dressing over cut sides of bread. Layer SPAM®, tomato, cheese, peppers, onion, olives and lettuce over bottom of loaf. Cover with top half of bread; press down to make a compact sandwich. Wrap in foil. Refrigerate 2 hours. Cut crosswise to serve. *Makes 6 servings*

# chili dogs

½ pound lean ground beef
1 cup chopped onions
1 can (6 ounces) HUNT'S® Tomato Paste No Salt Added
1 cup water
2 tablespoons GEBHARDT® Chili Powder
1 tablespoon prepared yellow mustard
½ teaspoon garlic powder
½ teaspoon ground cumin
¼ teaspoon sugar
⅛ teaspoon crushed red pepper
1 pound BUTTERBALL® Turkey Franks
10 hot dog buns

In skillet, brown beef and onions. Stir in tomato paste, water, chili powder, mustard, garlic powder, cumin, sugar and crushed red pepper; heat through. Meanwhile, heat or grill hot dogs. To serve, place hot dogs in buns; spoon chili down center of each. *Makes 10 chili dogs*

# crunchy turkey pita pockets

1 cup diced cooked turkey or chicken breast
   or reduced-sodium deli turkey breast
½ cup packaged cole slaw mix
½ cup dried cranberries
¼ cup shredded carrots
2 tablespoons reduced-fat or fat-free mayonnaise
1 tablespoon honey mustard
2 whole wheat pita breads

1. Combine turkey, cole slaw mix, cranberries, carrots, mayonnaise and mustard in small bowl; mix well.

2. Cut pita breads in half; fill with turkey mixture.

*Makes 2 servings*

# ham tortillas with picante sauce

2 tablespoons mayonnaise or salad dressing
1 tablespoon picante sauce
2 (8-inch) flour tortillas, warmed
4 thin slices CURE 81® ham
   Shredded lettuce
   Chopped tomato

In small bowl, combine mayonnaise and picante sauce. Spread tortillas with mayonnaise mixture. Top each tortilla with two ham slices, lettuce and tomato. Roll up. Serve with additional picante sauce, if desired. *Makes 2 servings*

crunchy turkey pita pockets

# monster sandwiches

∙∙∙∙∙∙∙∙∙∙∙∙∙∙∙∙∙∙∙∙∙∙∙∙∙∙∙∙∙∙∙∙∙∙∙∙∙∙∙∙∙∙∙∙∙∙∙∙∙∙∙∙∙∙∙∙∙∙

    8 assorted round and oblong sandwich rolls
      Butter
16 to 24 slices assorted cold cuts (salami, turkey, ham,
      bologna)
  6 to 8 slices assorted cheeses (American, Swiss,
      Muenster)
    1 firm tomato, sliced
    1 cucumber, sliced thinly
      Assorted lettuce leaves (Romaine, curly, red leaf)
      Cocktail onions
      Green and black olives
      Cherry tomatoes
      Pickled gherkins
      Radishes
      Baby corn
      Hard-cooked eggs

1. Cut rolls open just below center and spread with butter.

2. Layer meats, cheeses, tomato and cucumber slices and greens to make monster faces. Roll "tongues" from ham slices or make "lips" with tomato slices.

3. Use toothpicks to affix remaining ingredients for eyes, ears, fins, horns, hair, etc. *Makes 8 sandwiches*

Note: Remember to remove toothpicks before eating.

**66**

monster sandwiches

# magnificent salsa meatball hoagies

1 (6.8-ounce) package RICE-A-RONI® Beef Flavor
1 pound ground beef
½ cup dry bread crumbs
1 (24-ounce) jar salsa, divided
1 large egg
6 hoagie or French rolls, split in half
    Grated Parmesan cheese (optional)

1. In large bowl, combine rice-vermicelli mix, ground beef, bread crumbs, ½ cup salsa, egg and Special Seasonings. Shape meat mixture into 24 (1½-inch) meatballs. Arrange in large skillet.

2. Add 1½ cups water and remaining salsa; bring to a boil. Reduce heat to medium. Cover; simmer 30 to 35 minutes or until rice in meatballs is tender.

3. Place 4 meatballs in each roll. Top with salsa mixture and cheese, if desired.                    *Makes 6 servings*

**Tip:** For an Italian flair, use spaghetti sauce instead of salsa.

**Prep Time:** 15 minutes
**Cook Time:** 35 minutes

# tuna supper sandwiches

2 cups shredded Cheddar cheese
⅓ cup chopped green onions, including tops
⅓ cup chopped red bell pepper
1 can (2¼ ounces) sliced ripe olives, drained
2 tablespoons minced fresh parsley
1 teaspoon curry powder
   Seasoned salt to taste
1 (7-ounce) pouch of STARKIST® Premium Albacore or
   Chunk Light Tuna
½ cup light mayonnaise
6 soft French rolls (7 inches *each*), halved lengthwise

In medium bowl, place cheese, onions, bell pepper, olives, parsley, curry powder and salt; mix lightly. Add tuna and mayonnaise; toss lightly with fork. Cover baking sheet with foil; place rolls on foil. Spread about ⅓ cup mixture on each half. Bake in 450°F oven 10 to 12 minutes or until tops are bubbling and beginning to brown. Cool slightly before serving. *Makes 12 servings*

**Prep Time:** 18 minutes
**Cook Time:** 12 minutes

# maple francheezies

········································································

    Mustard Spread (recipe follows)
¼ cup maple syrup
2 teaspoons garlic powder
1 teaspoon black pepper
½ teaspoon ground nutmeg
4 slices bacon
4 jumbo hot dogs
4 hot dog buns, split
½ cup (2 ounces) shredded Cheddar cheese

Prepare Mustard Spread; set aside.

Prepare grill for direct cooking.

Combine maple syrup, garlic powder, pepper and nutmeg in small bowl. Brush syrup mixture onto bacon slices. Wrap 1 slice bacon around each hot dog.

Brush hot dogs with remaining syrup mixture. Place hot dogs on grid. Grill, covered, over medium-high heat 8 minutes or until bacon is crisp and hot dogs are heated through, turning halfway through grilling time. Place hot dogs in buns, top with Mustard Spread and cheese. *Makes 4 servings*

## FOOD CLUES

Maple syrup comes from the sap of certain species of maple trees. A tap inserted into the tree trunk during sugaring season drains the sap, which is then boiled and concentrated to form the thick, sweet liquid known as maple syrup.

## mustard spread

  ½ cup prepared yellow mustard
  1 tablespoon finely chopped onion
  1 tablespoon diced tomato
  1 tablespoon chopped fresh parsley
  1 teaspoon garlic powder
  ½ teaspoon black pepper

Combine all ingredients in small bowl; mix well.

*Makes about ¾ cup*

maple francheezy

# monster finger sandwiches

······························································

        1 can (11 ounces) refrigerated breadstick dough
             (12 breadsticks)
          Mustard
      12 slices deli ham, cut into ½-inch strips
        4 slices Monterey Jack cheese, cut into ½-inch strips
        1 egg yolk, lightly beaten
          Assorted food colorings

1. Preheat oven to 350°F. Place 6 breadsticks on ungreased baking sheets. Spread with mustard as desired. Divide ham strips evenly among breadsticks, placing over mustard. Repeat with cheese. Top with remaining 6 breadsticks. Gently stretch top dough over filling; press doughs together to seal.

2. Score knuckle and nail lines into each sandwich using sharp knife. Do not cut completely through dough. Tint egg yolk with food coloring as desired. Paint nail with egg yolk mixture.

3. Bake on lower oven rack 12 to 13 minutes or just until light golden. Let cool slightly. Serve warm or cool completely.

*Makes 6 servings*

monster finger sandwiches

# sloppy goblins

1 pound 90% lean ground beef
1 cup chopped onion
5 hot dogs, cut into ½-inch pieces
½ cup ketchup
¼ cup chopped dill pickle
¼ cup honey
¼ cup tomato paste
¼ cup prepared mustard
2 teaspoons cider vinegar
1 teaspoon Worcestershire sauce
8 hamburger buns
   Decorations: green olives, ripe olives, banana pepper
      slices, carrot curls and crinkles, red pepper, parsley
      sprigs and pretzel sticks

1. Cook beef and onion in large skillet over medium heat until beef is brown and onion is tender; drain. Stir in remaining ingredients except buns and decorations. Cook, covered, 5 minutes or until heated through.

2. Spoon meat mixture onto bottoms of buns; cover with tops of buns. Serve with decorations and let each person create a goblin face. Refrigerate leftovers.     *Makes 8 servings*

sloppy goblin

# cartoona sandwiches

½ cup low-fat mayonnaise
½ cup plain low-fat yogurt
1½ teaspoons curry powder (optional)
1 cup SUN-MAID® Raisins or Fruit Bits
½ cup diced celery or red bell pepper
1 green onion, thinly sliced
1 large can (12 ounces) tuna packed in water *or*
    1¼ cups chopped cooked chicken (2 small
    chicken breasts)
6 sandwich rolls, round or oblong shaped

1. **MAKE FILLING:** Mix in medium bowl mayonnaise, yogurt, curry powder, if desired, Sun-Maid® Raisins or Fruit Bits, celery or bell pepper, and green onion. Stir in tuna or chicken.

2. **MAKE "CAR":** Cut* ½-inch slice off top of a roll. With fingers or a fork, scoop out bread from center of roll.

3. **ATTACH** Sun-Maid® Apricots, carrot slices or other round ingredients to toothpick to make car "wheels." Insert wheels into bottom edge of roll. Add apple slices for "fenders," if desired.

4. **MAKE** "headlights" using toothpicks to attach raisins on one end of roll. Cut "doors" in sides of roll, if desired.

5. **FILL** roll with about ½ cup tuna or chicken salad. Place roll top on top of "car." Repeat with remaining rolls.

*Makes 6 sandwiches*

*Adult supervision is suggested.*

**Note:** Remove all toothpicks before eating.

**Prep Time:** 20 minutes

# chicken dogs on a stick

        1 tube (8 ounces) refrigerated crescent dinner rolls
           (8 rolls)
        1 pound boneless skinless chicken breast halves
        3 tablespoons CRISCO® Oil*
      ¾ cup shredded Romano cheese
        1 package (3 ounces) cream cheese, softened
      ¼ cup chopped onion
        3 tablespoons grated Parmesan cheese
      ¼ teaspoon Italian seasoning
      ¼ teaspoon pepper
        8 frozen treat sticks

*Use your favorite Crisco Oil product.*

Heat oven to 375°F.

Separate roll dough into triangles. Stretch each triangle into rectangle about 4 inches long.

Rinse chicken; pat dry. Cut into small cubes. Heat oil in medium skillet on high heat. Add chicken. Stir-fry about 3 minutes or until no longer pink in center. Drain. Cool.

Combine Romano cheese, cream cheese, onion, Parmesan cheese, Italian seasoning, pepper and chicken in medium bowl. Mix well. Spoon about ⅓ cup filling onto each dough rectangle. Wrap around wooden stick so that one end of stick can be used as "handle." Press and pinch dough ends to seal.

Bake for 15 to 20 minutes or until browned. Cool on rack 5 to 10 minutes before serving.                    *Makes 8 servings*

## sub on the run

  2 hard rolls (2 ounces each), split into halves
  4 tomato slices
14 turkey pepperoni slices
  2 ounces fat-free oven-roasted turkey breast
¼ cup (1 ounce) shredded part-skim mozzarella or
     reduced-fat sharp Cheddar cheese
  1 cup packaged coleslaw mix or shredded lettuce
¼ medium green bell pepper, thinly sliced (optional)
  2 tablespoons prepared fat-free Italian salad dressing

Top each of two bottom halves of rolls with 2 tomato slices,
7 pepperoni slices, half of turkey, 2 tablespoons cheese, ½ cup
coleslaw mix and half of bell pepper slices, if desired. Drizzle
each with 1 tablespoon salad dressing. Top with roll tops. Cut
into halves, if desired. *Makes 2 servings*

# FOOD CLUES

Mozzarella is a soft white cheese that melts easily.
In southern Italy, where it originated, it is made
from the milk of buffaloes. In other parts of Italy
and in North America, it is made from cow's milk.

sub on the run

# peanut butter and fruit pita pockets

1 large crisp apple, peeled, cored and finely diced
1 medium Bartlett pear, peeled, cored and finely diced
1½ teaspoons raisins
2 teaspoons orange juice
3 tablespoons super chunk peanut butter
4 large lettuce leaves or 8 large spinach leaves
2 whole wheat pitas, about 2 ounces each

**1.** Combine diced apples, pears and raisins with orange juice and hold for 5 minutes. Add peanut butter and mix well.

**2.** Wash and dry lettuce or spinach leaves on absorbant paper towels. Tear lettuce into pita size pieces.

**3.** Warm pita in toaster on lowest color setting. Cut pita in half, and carefully open each half to make a pocket.

**4.** Line each pocket with lettuce or spinach leaves and spoon in equal portions of fruit and peanut butter mixture. Serve and enjoy.                    *Makes 4 snack portions or 2 meal portions*

Favorite recipe from **Chilean Fresh Fruit Association**

## F OD CLUES

A delicious and fun snack kids of all ages can make
and enjoy...Sh-h-h-h, it's super healthy!

# corny sloppy joes

1 pound lean ground beef or ground turkey
1 small onion, chopped
1 can (15½ ounces) sloppy joe sauce
1 box (10 ounces) BIRDS EYE® frozen Sweet Corn
6 hamburger buns

• In large skillet, cook beef and onion over high heat until beef is well browned.

• Stir in sloppy joe sauce and corn; reduce heat to low and simmer 5 minutes or until heated through.

• Serve mixture in hamburger buns.          *Makes 6 servings*

**Serving Suggestion:** Sprinkle with shredded Cheddar cheese.

**Prep Time:** 5 minutes
**Cook Time:** 15 minutes

# come and get it!!

Kids will come running when they know exciting and fun meals, like Chuckwagon BBQ Rice Round-Up and Chicken Gigglers, are on the table. So give that dinner bell a jingle and be ready for the stampede.

# mini chicken pot pies

1 container (about 16 ounces) refrigerated reduced-fat
    buttermilk biscuits
1½ cups milk
1 package (1.8 ounces) white sauce mix
2 cups cut-up cooked chicken
1 cup frozen assorted vegetables, partially thawed
2 cups shredded Cheddar cheese
2 cups *French's*® French Fried Onions

1. Preheat oven to 400°F. Separate biscuits; press into
8 (8-ounce) custard cups, pressing up sides to form crust.

2. Whisk milk and sauce mix in medium saucepan. Bring to
boiling over medium-high heat. Reduce heat to medium-low;
simmer 1 minute, whisking constantly, until thickened. Stir in
chicken and vegetables.

3. Spoon about ⅓ cup chicken mixture into each crust. Place
cups on baking sheet. Bake 15 minutes or until golden brown.
Top each with cheese and French Fried Onions. Bake 3 minutes
or until golden. To serve, remove from cups and transfer to
serving plates.                              *Makes 8 servings*

**Prep Time:** 15 minutes
**Cook Time:** about 20 minutes

# chuckwagon bbq rice round-up

1 pound lean ground beef
1 (6.8-ounce) package RICE-A-RONI® Beef Flavor
2 tablespoons margarine or butter
2 cups frozen corn
½ cup prepared barbecue sauce
½ cup (2 ounces) shredded Cheddar cheese

1. In large skillet over medium-high heat, brown ground beef until well cooked. Remove from skillet; drain. Set aside.

2. In same skillet over medium heat, sauté rice-vermicelli mix with margarine until vermicelli is golden brown.

3. Slowly stir in 2½ cups water, corn and Special Seasonings; bring to a boil. Reduce heat to low. Cover; simmer 15 to 20 minutes or until rice is tender.

4. Stir in barbecue sauce and ground beef. Sprinkle with cheese. Cover; let stand 3 to 5 minutes or until cheese is melted.                                    *Makes 4 servings*

**Tip:** Salsa can be substituted for barbecue sauce.

**Prep Time:** 5 minutes
**Cook Time:** 25 minutes

chuckwagon bbq rice round-up

# zippity hot doggity tacos

1 small onion, finely chopped
1 tablespoon *Frank's® RedHot®* Original Cayenne Pepper
      Sauce or *French's®* Worcestershire Sauce
4 frankfurters, chopped
1 can (10½ ounces) red kidney or black beans, drained
1 can (8 ounces) tomato sauce
1 teaspoon chili powder
8 taco shells, heated
   Garnish: chopped tomatoes, shredded lettuce, sliced
      olives, sour cream, shredded cheese
1 cup *French's®* French Fried Onions

1. Heat *1 tablespoon oil* in 12-inch nonstick skillet over medium-high heat. Cook onion, 3 minutes or until crisp-tender. Stir in **Frank's RedHot** Sauce, frankfurters, beans, tomato sauce and chili powder. Bring to boiling. Reduce heat to medium-low and cook 5 minutes, stirring occasionally.

2. To serve, spoon chili into taco shells. Garnish as desired and sprinkle with French Fried Onions. Splash on **Frank's RedHot** Sauce for extra zip!                    *Makes 4 servings*

**Prep Time:** 5 minutes
**Cook Time:** 8 minutes

zippity hot doggity tacos

## corn dogs

........................................................................................

   8 wooden craft sticks
   8 hot dogs
   1 package (about 16 ounces) refrigerated grand-size
       corn biscuits
   ⅓ cup *French's*® Classic Yellow® Mustard
   8 slices American cheese, cut in half

1. Preheat oven to 350°F. Insert 1 wooden craft stick halfway into each hot dog; set aside.

2. Separate biscuits. On floured board, press or roll each biscuit into a 7×4-inch oval. Spread *2 teaspoons* mustard lengthwise down center of each biscuit. Top each with 2 pieces of cheese. Place hot dog in center of biscuit. Fold top of dough over end of hot dog. Fold sides towards center enclosing hot dog. Pinch edges to seal.

3. Place corn dogs, seam-side down, on greased baking sheet. Bake 20 to 25 minutes or until golden brown. Cool slightly before serving.                    *Makes 8 servings*

**Tip:** Corn dogs may be made without wooden craft sticks.

**Prep Time:** 15 minutes
**Cook Time:** 20 minutes

corn dogs

# terrifying tamale pie

1 tablespoon vegetable oil
½ cup chopped onion
⅓ cup chopped red bell pepper
1 clove garlic, minced
¾ pound ground turkey
¾ teaspoon chili powder
½ teaspoon dried oregano leaves
1 can (14½ ounces) Mexican-style stewed tomatoes, undrained
1 can (15 ounces) chili beans in mild chili sauce, undrained
1 cup corn
¼ teaspoon black pepper
1 package (8½ ounces) corn muffin mix plus ingredients to prepare mix
2 cups taco-flavored shredded cheese, divided
Green and red bell pepper, pickle slices, pimiento pieces, chopped onion, chopped black olives and carrots for decoration

1. Heat oil in large skillet over medium heat. Add onion and bell pepper; cook until crisp-tender. Stir in garlic. Add turkey; cook until turkey is no longer pink, stirring occasionally. Stir in chili powder and oregano. Add tomatoes with juice; cook and stir 2 minutes, breaking up tomatoes with spoon. Stir in beans with sauce, corn and black pepper; simmer 10 minutes or until liquid is reduced by about half.

2. Preheat oven to 375°F. Lightly grease 1½- to 2-quart casserole. Prepare corn muffin mix according to package directions; stir in ½ cup cheese. Spread half of turkey mixture in prepared casserole; sprinkle with ¾ cup cheese. Top with remaining turkey mixture and ¾ cup cheese. Top with corn

muffin batter. Decorate with assorted vegetables to make monster face. Bake 20 to 22 minutes or until light golden brown. *Makes 6 to 8 servings*

**Note:** Make this pie cute instead of creepy by creating a simple jack-o'-lantern face with bell pepper cutouts.

terrifying tamale pie

# chicken enchilada skillet casserole

1 bag (16 ounces) BIRDS EYE® frozen Farm Fresh
   Mixtures Broccoli, Corn & Red Peppers
3 cups shredded cooked chicken
1 can (16 ounces) diced tomatoes, undrained
1 package (1¼ ounces) taco seasoning mix
1 cup shredded Monterey Jack cheese
8 ounces tortilla chips

• In large skillet, combine vegetables, chicken, tomatoes and seasoning mix; bring to boil over medium-high heat.

• Cover; cook 4 minutes or until vegetables are cooked and mixture is heated through.

• Sprinkle with cheese; cover and cook 2 minutes more or until cheese is melted.

• Serve with chips. *Makes 4 servings*

**Prep Time:** 5 minutes
**Cook Time:** 10 minutes

FOOD CLUES

Enchiladas are Mexican entrées prepared by rolling
softened corn tortillas around a filling of shredded
meat, chicken or cheese.

chicken enchilada skillet casserole

# ham & cheese shells & trees

2 tablespoons margarine or butter
1 (6.2-ounce) package PASTA RONI® Shells & White
    Cheddar
2 cups fresh or frozen chopped broccoli
⅔ cup milk
1½ cups ham or cooked turkey, cut into thin strips (about
    6 ounces)

1. In large saucepan, bring 2 cups water and margarine to a boil.

2. Stir in pasta. Reduce heat to medium. Gently boil, uncovered, 6 minutes, stirring occasionally. Stir in broccoli; return to a boil. Boil 6 to 8 minutes or until most of water is absorbed.

3. Stir in milk, ham and Special Seasonings. Return to a boil; boil 1 to 2 minutes or until pasta is tender. Let stand 5 minutes before serving.                    *Makes 4 servings*

**Tip:** No leftovers? Ask the deli to slice a ½-inch-thick piece of ham or turkey.

**Prep Time:** 5 minutes
**Cook Time:** 20 minutes

ham & cheese shells & trees

# kid's choice meatballs

1½ pounds ground beef
¼ cup dry seasoned bread crumbs
¼ cup grated Parmesan cheese
3 tablespoons *French's®* Worcestershire Sauce
1 egg
2 jars (14 ounces each) spaghetti sauce

1. Preheat oven to 425°F. In bowl, gently mix beef, bread crumbs, cheese, Worcestershire and egg. Shape into 1-inch meatballs. Place on rack in roasting pan. Bake 15 minutes or until cooked.

2. In large saucepan, combine meatballs and spaghetti sauce. Cook until heated through. Serve over cooked pasta.
*Makes 6 to 8 servings (about 48 meatballs)*

**Quick Meatball Tip:** On waxed paper, pat meat mixture into 8×6×1-inch rectangle. With knife, cut crosswise and lengthwise into 1-inch rows. Roll each small square into a ball.

**Prep Time:** 10 minutes
**Cook Time:** 20 minutes

kid's choice meatballs

# chicken gigglers

1 pound chicken breast tenders*
¾ teaspoon salt
½ teaspoon dried parsley flakes *or* 1½ teaspoons chopped fresh parsley
¼ teaspoon ground sage *or* ¾ teaspoon chopped fresh sage
¼ teaspoon ground thyme leaves *or* ¾ teaspoon chopped fresh thyme
2 cups CRISCO® Oil**
1 box (7½ to 8½ ounces) yellow corn muffin mix
2 tablespoons finely chopped sweet onion
½ teaspoon dried basil leaves *or* 1½ teaspoons chopped fresh basil
⅔ cup milk
Mildly spiced dipping sauce

*If chicken tenders are not available, purchase chicken breasts and cut into strips.*

**Use your favorite Crisco Oil product.*

Rinse chicken; pat dry. Place in 8-inch square glass baking dish. Combine salt, parsley, sage and thyme. Sprinkle over chicken. Toss to coat.

Heat oil in deep skillet on medium heat.

Combine muffin mix, onion and basil in small bowl. Add milk. Stir until well blended. Coat chicken with batter. Drop pieces, 4 at a time, into hot oil. Fry for 2 minutes. Turn. Fry for 1 to 2 minutes or until no longer pink in center. Place on paper-towel lined plate. Keep warm until all chicken is fried. Serve warm with dipping sauce.                    *Makes 4 servings*

# cheeseburger macaroni

1 cup mostaccioli or elbow macaroni, uncooked
1 pound ground beef
1 medium onion, chopped
1 can (14½ ounces) DEL MONTE® Diced Tomatoes with
    Basil, Garlic & Oregano
¼ cup DEL MONTE® Tomato Ketchup
1 cup (4 ounces) shredded Cheddar cheese

1. Cook pasta according to package directions; drain.

2. Brown meat with onion in large skillet; drain. Season with salt and pepper, if desired. Stir in undrained tomatoes, ketchup and pasta; heat through.

3. Top with cheese. Garnish, if desired.     *Makes 4 servings*

**Prep Time:** 8 minutes
**Cook Time:** 15 minutes

## FOOD CLUES

A skillet, also known as a frying pan, is a round, shallow pan with a straight or slightly sloping side. It is used for frying and sautéing. Choose a heavy pan that conducts heat evenly and has a tight-fitting cover. Skillets range in size from 6 to 12 inches. A large skillet with a second short handle opposite the long handle is much easier to lift.

# western wagon wheels

1 pound lean ground beef or ground turkey
2 cups wagon wheel pasta, uncooked
1 can (14½ ounces) stewed tomatoes
1½ cups water
1 box (10 ounces) BIRDS EYE® frozen Sweet Corn
½ cup barbecue sauce
   Salt and pepper to taste

• In large skillet, cook beef over medium heat 5 minutes or until well browned.

• Stir in pasta, tomatoes, water, corn and barbecue sauce; bring to a boil.

• Reduce heat to low; cover and simmer 15 to 20 minutes or until pasta is tender, stirring occasionally. Season with salt and pepper.                                    *Makes 4 servings*

**Serving Suggestion:** Serve with corn bread or corn muffins.

**Prep Time:** 5 minutes
**Cook Time:** 25 minutes

western wagon wheels

# the best for last

Dessert Nachos, Chocolate Pudding Parfait or a Cookie Pizza Cake are just a few ways to convince kids that dessert is worth waiting for!

# cookie pizza cake

1 package (18 ounces) refrigerated chocolate chip
    cookie dough
1 package (16 to 18 ounces) chocolate cake mix, plus
    ingredients to prepare
1 cup prepared vanilla frosting
½ cup peanut butter
1 to 2 tablespoons milk
1 container (16 ounces) chocolate frosting
    Chocolate peanut butter cups or other candy pieces
    (optional)

1. Preheat oven to 350°F. Coat two 12-inch round pizza pans with nonstick cooking spray. Press cookie dough evenly onto one pan. Bake 15 to 20 minutes or until edges are golden brown. Cool 20 minutes in pan on wire rack. Loosen edges of cookie with knife. Turn pan over to release cookie. Set aside.

2. Prepare cake mix according to package directions. Fill second pan ¼ to ½ full with batter. (Reserve remaining cake mix for another use, such as cupcakes.) Bake 10 to 15 minutes or until toothpick inserted into center comes out clean. Cool 15 minutes on wire rack. Gently remove cake from pan; cool completely.

3. Combine vanilla frosting and peanut butter in small bowl. Gradually stir in milk, 1 tablespoon at a time, until of spreadable consistency.

4. Place cookie on serving plate. Spread peanut butter frosting on top of cookie. Place cake on top of cookie, trimming cookie to match size of cake, if necessary. Frost top and side of cake with chocolate frosting. Decorate with peanut butter cups, if desired. Cut into slices.

*Makes 12 to 14 servings*

# frozen berry ice cream

        8 ounces frozen unsweetened strawberries, partially
            thawed
        8 ounces frozen unsweetened peaches, partially thawed
        4 ounces frozen unsweetened blueberries, partially
            thawed
        6 packets sugar substitute
        2 teaspoons vanilla
        2 cups no-sugar-added light vanilla ice cream
       16 blueberries
        4 small strawberries, halved
        8 peach slices

1. Combine frozen strawberries, peaches, blueberries, sugar substitute and vanilla in food processor. Process until coarsely chopped.

2. Add ice cream; process until well blended.

3. Serve immediately for semi-soft texture or freeze until needed and allow to stand 10 minutes to soften slightly. Garnish each serving with 2 blueberries for "eyes," 1 strawberry half for "nose" and 1 peach slice for "smile."

*Makes 8 servings (½ cup each)*

frozen berry ice cream

# candy corn crispie treats

........................................................................

½ cup (1 stick) butter or margarine
9 cups miniature marshmallows
10 cups chocolate crispy rice cereal
2 cups candy corn
¾ cup miniature chocolate chips
    Assorted candy pumpkins

1. Melt butter in large saucepan over medium heat. Add marshmallows and stir until smooth.

2. Pour cereal, candy corn and chocolate chips into large bowl. Pour butter and marshmallows over cereal mixture, stirring quickly to coat. For best results, use a wooden spoon sprayed with nonstick cooking spray.

3. Spread mixture on large buttered jelly-roll pan, pressing out evenly with buttered hands. While still warm, press on candy pumpkins spaced about 1½ inches apart.

4. Cool, then cut into squares.        *Makes about 48 squares*

# caramel apple wedges

........................................................................

⅔ cup sugar
¼ cup (½ stick) butter, cut into small pieces
½ cup whipping cream
¼ teaspoon salt
3 apples, cored and cut into 6 wedges
½ cup shredded coconut
¼ cup mini chocolate chips

1. Place sugar in medium, heavy saucepan. Cook over low heat until sugar melts, about 20 minutes. Carefully stir in butter then cream. (Mixture will spatter.) Cook over low heat until any lumps disappear, about 15 minutes, stirring occasionally. Stir in salt.

**2.** To serve, pour caramel sauce into serving bowl or fondue pot over heat source. Arrange apple wedges on plate. Combine coconut and chocolate chips in separate serving dish.

**3.** Using fondue forks, dip apple wedges into caramel sauce, then into coconut mixture.                *Makes 6 servings*

**Variation:** To make caramel apples, combine 1 package (14 ounces) caramels and 2 tablespoons water in heavy saucepan. Melt over low heat, about 10 minutes. Roll apples in melted caramel mixture, then in coconut mixture. Cool on sheet of waxed paper until firm.

caramel apple wedges

# rich chocolate pudding

⅔ cup sugar
¼ cup unsweetened cocoa powder
3 tablespoons cornstarch
2 cups reduced-fat (2%) milk
1 egg
½ teaspoon vanilla
1 tablespoon butter

1. Combine sugar, cocoa and cornstarch in medium saucepan; whisk in milk. Cook over medium-high heat, stirring frequently, until mixture boils; boil 1 minute, stirring constantly.

2. Beat egg in small bowl. Whisk about ½ cup hot milk mixture into egg; whisk egg mixture back into saucepan. Cook over medium heat 2 minutes, stirring constantly.

3. Remove pudding from heat; stir in vanilla and butter. Pour into 4 individual serving dishes. Serve warm or cover and refrigerate until ready to serve.          *Makes 4 servings*

**Rich Mocha Pudding:** Add 1 to 1½ teaspoons instant coffee crystals to sugar mixture in step 1.

**Serving Suggestion:** Serve pudding with banana slices, mandarin orange segments and cookies. Or top with scoops of ice cream or frozen yogurt and a sprinkle of grated chocolate.

rich chocolate pudding

# peanut butter s'more sundae

Vanilla ice cream
REESE'S® Shell Topping®
Marshmallow creme
HERSHEY'S Syrup
REDDI-WIP® Whipped Topping
Maraschino cherry
Graham crackers or animal crackers

• Place ice cream in sundae dish.

• Top with REESE'S Shell Topping, marshmallow creme, HERSHEY'S Syrup, REDDI-WIP Whipped Topping and maraschino cherry.

• Decorate with graham crackers or animal crackers.

*Makes 1 sundae*

# sundae pie

1 (16-ounce) can dark sweet cherries, drained
1 (9-inch) baked pie shell
4 cups vanilla ice cream, softened
½ cup chocolate ice cream topping
½ cup chopped pecans

Place one-half of cherries in baked pie shell; top with 2 cups ice cream. Drizzle ⅓ cup chocolate topping over ice cream. Add remaining cherries. Sprinkle pecans on top. Spoon remaining ice cream evenly over pie. Drizzle with remaining chocolate topping.

Freeze several hours or overnight. Let thaw 5 to 10 minutes before serving. Garnish with whipped cream and maraschino cherries, if desired. *Makes 8 servings*

Favorite recipe from *Cherry Marketing Institute*

# caramel apples

2 cups heavy cream
2 cups sugar
¼ Butter Flavor CRISCO® Stick or ¼ cup Butter Flavor
    CRISCO® Shortening
½ cup dark corn syrup
12 wooden craft sticks*
12 medium McIntosh apples, washed and stemmed

*Use 5-inch craft sticks, ¼-inch in diameter.

Line baking sheet with parchment paper; set aside. Fill about half of a large bowl with ice water.

Place cream, sugar, CRISCO® Shortening and corn syrup in a heavy-bottomed saucepan; bring to a boil over medium heat. Continue cooking until the temperature registers 245°F on a candy thermometer, 10 to 12 minutes. Remove from heat and briefly plunge the saucepan into ice water to stop the caramel from cooking. Remove from ice water and let mixture cool for a few minutes.

Insert a craft stick into the stem end of each apple. Dip 1 apple into the caramel; coat the top and sides with caramel using a spoon. Transfer to prepared baking sheet to cool. Repeat with remaining apples. Garnish as desired, or serve in seasonal cupcake liners. *Makes 12 apples*

**Optional Toppings:** Chocolate covered toffee bits, crushed Macadamia nuts, crushed peanuts, seasonal sprinkles, tinted coconut or chopped candy corn.

# banana smoothies & pops

1 (14-ounce) can EAGLE BRAND® Sweetened
    Condensed Milk (NOT evaporated milk)
1 (8-ounce) container vanilla yogurt
2 ripe bananas
½ cup orange juice

1. In blender container, combine all ingredients; blend until smooth. Stop occasionally to scrape down sides.

2. Serve immediately. Store covered in refrigerator.

*Makes 4 cups*

**Banana Smoothie Pops:** Spoon banana mixture into 8 (5-ounce) paper cups. Freeze 30 minutes. Insert wooden craft sticks into the center of each cup; freeze until firm. Makes 8 pops.

**Fruit Smoothies:** Substitute 1 cup of your favorite fruit and ½ cup any fruit juice for banana and orange juice.

**Prep Time:** 5 minutes

banana smoothie & pops

# oatmeal cookie ice cream sandwiches

........................................................................

1 cup all-purpose flour
1 teaspoon baking powder
½ teaspoon salt
½ cup unsalted butter
1 cup packed dark brown sugar
1 egg, beaten
1 teaspoon vanilla
1 cup quick-cooking oats
½ cup chopped walnuts
1½ pints pumpkin or maple-walnut ice cream
   Black and orange jimmies, sugar or other Halloween
   cookie decorations (optional)

1. Preheat oven to 350°F. Grease cookie sheets. Combine flour, baking powder and salt in medium bowl.

2. Beat butter and sugar in bowl of electric mixer until light and fluffy. Add egg and vanilla; beat until well blended. Add flour mixture, a few tablespoons at a time, beating until well blended. Stir in oats and walnuts.

3. Scoop dough by rounded tablespoonfuls and place 2 inches apart onto prepared cookie sheets to make 24 cookies. Flatten dough to ½-inch thickness.

4. Bake 15 to 20 minutes or until lightly brown. Cool on cookie sheets 5 minutes. Remove to wire rack. Cool completely.

5. Soften ice cream at room temperature about 10 minutes or in microwave oven at MEDIUM (50% power) 10 to 20 seconds. For each ice cream sandwich, place about ¼ cup

(1 small scoop) ice cream on flat side of one cookie; top with another cookie, flat side down. Press gently so that ice cream meets edges of cookies. Immediately roll edges of ice cream in decorations, if desired. Wrap in plastic wrap; freeze until ready to serve.

*Makes 12 sandwiches*

# quick chocolate pudding

¼ cup unsweetened cocoa powder
2 tablespoons cornstarch
1½ cups reduced-fat (2%) milk
6 to 8 packets sugar substitute or equivalent of ⅓ cup sugar
1 teaspoon vanilla
⅛ teaspoon ground cinnamon (optional)
Assorted sugar-free candies (optional)

**1.** Combine cocoa powder and cornstarch in medium microwavable bowl or 1-quart glass measure. Gradually whisk in milk until well blended.

**2.** Microwave at HIGH 2 minutes; stir. Microwave at MEDIUM-HIGH (70% power) 3 to 4½ minutes or until thickened, stirring every 1½ minutes.

**3.** Stir in sugar substitute, vanilla and cinnamon, if desired. Let stand at least 5 minutes before serving, stirring occasionally to prevent skin from forming. Serve warm or chilled. Garnish with candies just before serving, if desired.

*Makes 4 servings*

# creamy strawberry-banana tart

1 (16-ounce) package frozen unsweetened whole
    strawberries, thawed
2 tablespoons plus 1½ teaspoons frozen orange juice
    concentrate, thawed, divided
¼ cup sugar
1 envelope unflavored gelatin
3 egg whites, beaten
1 (3-ounce) package soft ladyfingers, split
4 teaspoons water
½ (8-ounce) container frozen reduced-fat whipped
    dessert topping, thawed
1 medium banana, quartered lengthwise and sliced
1 teaspoon multi-colored decorator sprinkles (optional)

1. Place strawberries and 2 tablespoons orange juice concentrate in blender container or food processor bowl. Blend or process until smooth.

2. Stir together sugar and gelatin in medium saucepan. Stir in strawberry mixture. Cook, stirring frequently, until mixture comes to a boil. Stir about half of mixture into beaten egg whites. Return all to saucepan. Cook, stirring constantly, over medium heat about 2 minutes or until slightly thickened. *(Do not boil.)*

3. Pour into bowl. Refrigerate 2 to 2½ hours or until mixture mounds when spooned, stirring occasionally.

4. Cut half of ladyfingers in half horizontally. Place around edge of 9-inch tart pan with removable bottom. Place remaining ladyfingers in bottom of pan, cutting to fit.

5. Stir together remaining 1½ teaspoons orange juice concentrate and water. Drizzle over ladyfingers.

6. Fold dessert topping and banana into strawberry mixture. Spoon into ladyfinger crust. Refrigerate at least 2 hours. Decorate with sprinkles, if desired.    *Makes 10 servings*

creamy strawberry-banana tart

# dessert nachos

· · · · · · · · · · · · · · · · · · · · · · · · · · · · · · · · · · · · · · · · · · · · · ·

   3 (6- to 7-inch) flour tortillas
     Nonstick cooking spray
   1 tablespoon sugar
  ⅛ teaspoon ground cinnamon
     Dash ground allspice
   1 (6- or 8-ounce) container fat-free sugar-free
      vanilla yogurt
   1 teaspoon grated orange peel
1½ cups strawberries
  ½ cup blueberries
   4 teaspoons miniature semisweet chocolate chips

1. Preheat oven to 375°F.

2. Cut each flour tortilla into 8 wedges. Place on ungreased baking sheet. Generously spray tortilla wedges with cooking spray. Stir together sugar, cinnamon and allspice. Sprinkle over tortilla wedges. Bake 7 to 9 minutes or until lightly browned; cool completely.

3. Meanwhile, stir together yogurt and orange peel. Stem strawberries; cut lengthwise into fourths.

4. Place 6 tortilla wedges on each of 4 small plates. Top with strawberries and blueberries. Drizzle yogurt mixture on top. Sprinkle with chocolate chips. Serve immediately.

*Makes 4 servings*

dessert nachos

# peanut butter ice cream triangles

1½ cups all-purpose flour
½ teaspoon baking powder
½ teaspoon baking soda
¼ teaspoon salt
½ cup butter, softened
½ cup granulated sugar
½ cup packed brown sugar
½ cup creamy peanut butter
1 egg
1 teaspoon vanilla
2½ to 3 cups vanilla, cinnamon or chocolate ice cream,
softened

1. Preheat oven to 350°F. Grease cookie sheets.

2. Combine flour, baking powder, baking soda and salt in small bowl; set aside. Beat butter, granulated sugar and brown sugar in large bowl of electric mixer at medium speed until light and fluffy. Beat in peanut butter, egg and vanilla until well blended. Gradually beat in flour mixture on low speed until blended.

3. Divide dough in half. Roll each piece of dough between 2 sheets of waxed paper or plastic wrap into 10×10-inch square, about ⅛ inch thick. Remove top sheet of waxed paper; invert dough onto prepared cookie sheet. Remove second sheet of waxed paper.

4. Score dough into four 4-inch squares. Score each square diagonally into two triangles. *Do not cut completely through dough.* Repeat with remaining dough. Combine excess scraps of dough; roll out and score into additional triangles.

**5.** Bake 12 to 13 minutes or until set and edges are golden brown. Cool cookies 2 minutes on cookie sheets. Cut through score marks with knife; cool completely on cookie sheets.

**6.** Place half the cookies on flat surface. Spread ¼ to ⅓ cup ice cream on flat side of each cookie; top with remaining cookies. Wrap in plastic wrap and freeze 1 hour or up to 2 days.          *Makes about 10 ice cream sandwiches*

**peanut butter ice cream triangle**

# acknowledgments

*The publisher would like to thank the companies and organizations
listed below for the use of their recipes and photographs
in this publication.*

Birds Eye®

Bob Evans®

Cherry Marketing Institute

Chilean Fresh Fruit Association

ConAgra Foods®

Del Monte Corporation

Eagle Brand®

Egg Beaters®

The Golden Grain Company®

Hebrew National®

Hershey Foods Corporation

Hormel Foods, LLC

The Kingsford Products Company

© Mars, Incorporated 2004

National Honey Board

Nestlé USA

Norseland, Inc.Lucini Italia Co.

Reckitt Benckiser Inc.

Reddi-wip® is a registered trademark of ConAgra Brands, Inc.

The J.M. Smucker Company

Southeast United Dairy Industry Association, Inc.

StarKist® Seafood Company

Sun•Maid® Growers of California

**Apples**
Breakfast S'mores, 15
Caramel Apples, 111
Caramel Apple Wedges, 106
Ham 'n' Apple Rollers, 27
Old-Fashioned Caramel Apples, 45
Peanut Butter and Fruit Pita Pockets, 80

Backyard S'mores, 38
**Bananas**
Banana Freezer Pops, 32
Banana Smoothies & Pops, 112
Breakfast S'mores, 15
Creamy Strawberry-Banana Tart, 116
Frozen Banana Shakes, 32
Peanut Butter and Jelly Club Sandwich, 58
Peppy Purple Pops, 32
Barbecue Flying Saucers with Vegetable Martians, 60

**Beans**
Cheesy Barbecued Bean Dip, 44
Terrifying Tamale Pie, 90
Zippity Hot Doggity Tacos, 86

**Beef**
Bologna "Happy Faces," 58
Cheeseburger Macaroni, 99
Chili Dogs, 63
Chuckwagon BBQ Rice Round-Up, 84
Corny Sloppy Joes, 81
Kid's Choice Meatballs, 96
Magnificent Salsa Meatball Hoagies, 68
Sloppy Goblins, 74
Sloppy Joes, 62
Tacos Olé, 57
Western Wagon Wheels, 100

**Bell Peppers**
Cheesy Barbecued Bean Dip, 44
Hero SPAM™ Sandwich, 62
Tortellini Teasers, 48
Biscuits 'n Gravy, 14
**Blueberries**
Dessert Nachos, 118
Frozen Berry Ice Cream, 104
Snacking Surprise Muffins, 22
Bologna "Happy Faces," 58
Breakfast S'mores, 15
Brontosaurus Bites, 46
Butterscotch Nut Clusters, 36

Candy Corn Crispie Treats, 106
Caramel Apples, 111
Caramel Apple Wedges, 106
**Carrots**
Cheesy Barbecued Bean Dip, 44
Tortellini Teasers, 48
Cartoona Sandwiches, 76
**Cereal**
Brontosaurus Bites, 46
Cinnamon Trail Mix, 30
Gorilla Grub, 46
Kool-Pop Treat, 44
Sweet Nothings Trail Mix, 54
**Cheese**
Cheeseburger Macaroni, 99
Cheese Straws, 40
Cheesy Barbecued Bean Dip, 44
Chicken Dogs on a Stick, 77
Chicken Enchilada Skillet Casserole, 92
Chuckwagon BBQ Rice Round-Up, 84
Corn Dogs, 88
Ham 'n' Apple Rollers, 27

Hero SPAM™ Sandwich, 62
Maple Francheezies, 70
Mini Chicken Pot Pies, 83
Monster Finger Sandwiches, 72
Monster Sandwiches, 66
Monte Cristo Sandwiches, 18
Pizza for Breakfast, 8
Quick Pizza Snacks, 38
Rock 'n' Rollers, 27
Terrifying Tamale Pie, 90
Tuna Supper Sandwiches, 69
Cheesy Tooty Fruitys, 24
**Cherries**
Peanut Butter S'more Sundae, 110
Sundae Pie, 110
Sunday Morning Upside-Down Rolls, 10
Cherry-Peach Pops, 52
**Chicken**
Chicken Dogs on a Stick, 77
Chicken Enchilada Skillet Casserole, 92
Chicken Gigglers, 98
Mini Chicken Pot Pies, 83
Chili Dogs, 63
**Chocolate**
Backyard S'mores, 38
Candy Corn Crispie Treats, 106
Caramel Apple Wedges, 106
Chocolate Glaze, 17
Chocolate Raspberry, 43
Chocolate Waffles, 7
Clown-Around Cones, 34
Cookie Pizza Cake, 103
Dessert Nachos, 118
Green's "Dare to Dip 'em" Donuts, 16
Hershey's Easy Chocolate Cracker Snacks, 42
Peanut Butter and Milk Chocolate, 42

# index

Quick Chocolate Pudding, 115
Rich Chocolate Pudding, 108
Rich Mocha Pudding, 108
S'mores on a Stick, 28
Sundae Pie, 110
Sweet Nothings Trail Mix, 54
Toll House® Mini Morsel Pancakes, 12
Whip 'em Up Wacky Waffles, 7
Chuckwagon BBQ Rice Round-Up, 84
Cinnamon Trail Mix, 30
Clown-Around Cones, 34
Cookie Pizza Cake, 103
**Corn**
Chuckwagon BBQ Rice Round-Up, 84
Corny Sloppy Joes, 81
Terrifying Tamale Pie, 90
Western Wagon Wheels, 100
Corn Dogs, 88
Creamy Strawberry-Banana Tart, 116
Crunchy Turkey Pita Pockets, 64

Dessert Nachos, 118
Double Peanut Clusters, 36

Frozen Banana Shakes, 32
Frozen Berry Ice Cream, 104
**Frozen Mixed Vegetables**
Chicken Enchilada Skillet Casserole, 92
Mini Chicken Pot Pies, 83
Fruit Smoothies, 112

Gorilla Grub, 46
**Graham Crackers**
Backyard S'mores, 38
Brontosaurus Bites, 46
Gorilla Grub, 46
Peanut Butter S'more Sundae, 110
S'mores on a Stick, 28

Granola Crisp Topping with Fruit, 50
Green's "Dare to Dip 'em" Donuts, 16

**Ham**
Ham 'n' Apple Rollers, 27
Ham & Cheese Shells & Trees, 94
Ham Tortillas with Picante Sauce, 64
Monster Finger Sandwiches, 72
Monte Cristo Sandwiches, 18
Hero SPAM™ Sandwich, 62
Hershey's Easy Chocolate Cracker Snacks, 42
**Hot Dogs**
Chili Dogs, 63
Corn Dogs, 88
Maple Francheezies, 70
Sloppy Goblins, 74
Sweet and Sour Hot Dog Bites, 53
Zippity Hot Doggity Tacos, 86

**Ice Cream**
Clown-Around Cones, 34
Frozen Berry Ice Cream, 104
Oatmeal Cookie Ice Cream Sandwiches, 114
Peanut Butter Ice Cream Triangles, 120
Peanut Butter S'more Sundae, 110
Sundae Pie, 110

Jam French Toast Triangles, 20
**Juice from Concentrate**
Banana Freezer Pops, 32
Frozen Banana Shakes, 32
Peppy Purple Pops, 32

Kid's Choice Meatballs, 96
Kool-Pop Treat, 44

Magnificent Salsa Meatball Hoagies, 68
Maple Francheezies, 70
**Marshmallows**
Backyard S'mores, 38
Breakfast S'mores, 15
Candy Corn Crispie Treats, 106
Kool-Pop Treat, 44
S'mores on a Stick, 28
Mini Chicken Pot Pies, 83
Monster Finger Sandwiches, 72
Monster Sandwiches, 66
Monte Cristo Sandwiches, 18
**Mushrooms**
Pizza for Breakfast, 8
Tortellini Teasers, 48
Mustard Spread, 71

**Nuts**
Butterscotch Nut Clusters, 36
Double Peanut Clusters, 36
Oatmeal Cookie Ice Cream Sandwiches, 114
Sundae Pie, 110
Sweet Nothings Trail Mix, 54

Oatmeal Cookie Ice Cream Sandwiches, 114
Old-Fashioned Caramel Apples, 45

**Pasta**
Cheeseburger Macaroni, 99
Ham & Cheese Shells & Trees, 94
Tortellini Teasers, 48
Western Wagon Wheels, 100
**Peaches**
Cherry-Peach Pops, 52
Frozen Berry Ice Cream, 104

**Peanut Butter**
Cookie Pizza Cake, 103
Peanut Butter and Fruit Pita Pockets, 80
Peanut Butter and Jelly Club Sandwich, 58
Peanut Butter Ice Cream Triangles, 120
**Peanut Butter Chips**
Double Peanut Clusters, 36
Peanut Butter and Milk Chocolate, 42
Peanut Butter S'more Sundae, 110
Peppy Purple Pops, 32
**Pineapples**
Brontosaurus Bites, 46
Gorilla Grub, 46
Pizza for Breakfast, 8
**Popcorn**
Brontosaurus Bites, 46
Gorilla Grub, 46
Kool-Pop Treat, 44
**Pork**
Barbecue Flying Saucers with Vegetable Martians, 60
Hero SPAM™ Sandwich, 62

Quick Chocolate Pudding, 115
Quick Pizza Snacks, 38

**Raisins**
Brontosaurus Bites, 46
Cartoona Sandwiches, 76
Gorilla Grub, 46
Sweet Nothings Trail Mix, 54
Rich Chocolate Pudding, 108
Rich Mocha Pudding, 108
Rock 'n' Rollers, 27

S'mores on a Stick, 28
**Salsa**
Magnificent Salsa Meatball Hoagies, 68

Sassy Salsa Rollers, 27
Tacos Olé, 57
**Sausage**
Biscuits 'n Gravy, 14
Pizza for Breakfast, 8
Sausage Pinwheels, 20
Sloppy Goblins, 74
Sloppy Joes, 62
Snacking Surprise Muffins, 22
**Strawberries**
Creamy Strawberry-Banana Tart, 116
Dessert Nachos, 118
Frozen Berry Ice Cream, 104
Sub on the Run, 78
Sundae Pie, 110
Sunday Morning Upside-Down Rolls, 10
Sweet and Sour Hot Dog Bites, 53
Sweet Nothings Trail Mix, 54
Sweet Tooty Fruitys, 24

Tacos Olé, 57
Terrifying Tamale Pie, 90
Toll House® Mini Morsel Pancakes, 12
**Tomatoes**
Cheeseburger Macaroni, 99
Chicken Enchilada Skillet Casserole, 92
Hero SPAM™ Sandwich, 62
Monster Sandwiches, 66
Pizza for Breakfast, 8
Quick Pizza Snacks, 38
Sub on the Run, 78
Terrifying Tamale Pie, 90
Tortellini Teasers, 48
Vegetable Martians, 61
Western Wagon Wheels, 100
Zesty Tomato Sauce, 48
Tooty Fruitys, 24
Tortellini Teasers, 48

**Tuna**
Cartoona Sandwiches, 76
Tuna Supper Sandwiches, 69
**Turkey**
Crunchy Turkey Pita Pockets, 64
Monte Cristo Sandwiches, 18
Rock 'n' Rollers, 27
Sassy Salsa Rollers, 27
Sub on the Run, 78
Terrifying Tamale Pie, 90

Vegetable Martians, 61

Wedgies, 27
Western Wagon Wheels, 100
Whip 'em Up Wacky Waffles, 7
White Chip and Toffee, 43

**Yogurt**
Cartoona Sandwiches, 76
Cherry-Peach Pops, 52
Dessert Nachos, 118
Granola Crisp Topping with Fruit, 50

Zesty Tomato Sauce, 48
Zippity Hot Doggity Tacos, 86

# metric conversion chart

## VOLUME MEASUREMENTS (dry)

1/8 teaspoon = 0.5 mL
1/4 teaspoon = 1 mL
1/2 teaspoon = 2 mL
3/4 teaspoon = 4 mL
1 teaspoon = 5 mL
1 tablespoon = 15 mL
2 tablespoons = 30 mL
1/4 cup = 60 mL
1/3 cup = 75 mL
1/2 cup = 125 mL
2/3 cup = 150 mL
3/4 cup = 175 mL
1 cup = 250 mL
2 cups = 1 pint = 500 mL
3 cups = 750 mL
4 cups = 1 quart = 1 L

## VOLUME MEASUREMENTS (fluid)

1 fluid ounce (2 tablespoons) = 30 mL
4 fluid ounces (1/2 cup) = 125 mL
8 fluid ounces (1 cup) = 250 mL
12 fluid ounces (1 1/2 cups) = 375 mL
16 fluid ounces (2 cups) = 500 mL

## WEIGHTS (mass)

1/2 ounce = 15 g
1 ounce = 30 g
3 ounces = 90 g
4 ounces = 120 g
8 ounces = 225 g
10 ounces = 285 g
12 ounces = 360 g
16 ounces = 1 pound = 450 g

## DIMENSIONS

1/16 inch = 2 mm
1/8 inch = 3 mm
1/4 inch = 6 mm
1/2 inch = 1.5 cm
3/4 inch = 2 cm
1 inch = 2.5 cm

## OVEN TEMPERATURES

250°F = 120°C
275°F = 140°C
300°F = 150°C
325°F = 160°C
350°F = 180°C
375°F = 190°C
400°F = 200°C
425°F = 220°C
450°F = 230°C

## BAKING PAN SIZES

| Utensil | Size in Inches/Quarts | Metric Volume | Size in Centimeters |
|---|---|---|---|
| Baking or Cake Pan (square or rectangular) | 8×8×2 | 2 L | 20×20×5 |
| | 9×9×2 | 2.5 L | 23×23×5 |
| | 12×8×2 | 3 L | 30×20×5 |
| | 13×9×2 | 3.5 L | 33×23×5 |
| Loaf Pan | 8×4×3 | 1.5 L | 20×10×7 |
| | 9×5×3 | 2 L | 23×13×7 |
| Round Layer Cake Pan | 8×1½ | 1.2 L | 20×4 |
| | 9×1½ | 1.5 L | 23×4 |
| Pie Plate | 8×1¼ | 750 mL | 20×3 |
| | 9×1¼ | 1 L | 23×3 |
| Baking Dish or Casserole | 1 quart | 1 L | — |
| | 1½ quart | 1.5 L | — |
| | 2 quart | 2 L | — |